Cottage Cheese
Cookbook

Easy High-Protein, Low-Carb, and Delicious
Cottage Cheese Recipes for Beginners

Gloria Caldwell

Copyright © [2024] by Gloria Caldwell

TWO BONUSES FOR YOU!

- Global flavors
- Shopping list essentials

Special Note of Thanks to Sophia Martinez and Dr. James Carter

I would like to extend my deepest gratitude to Sophia Martinez, a licensed dietitian whose expertise and passion for nutrition were integral to the creation of this book. Sophia's dedication to balanced, wholesome eating ensured that each recipe not only tastes delicious but also offers optimal nutrition. Her insight into incorporating cottage cheese into everyday meals has elevated this collection, making it a trusted resource for health-conscious home cooks.

A special thanks also goes to Dr. James Carter, a seasoned nutrition scientist with over 20 years of experience in the field of food science and dietary research. Dr. Carter's extensive background in developing nutrient-dense recipes and his understanding of the latest research in functional foods brought a cutting-edge perspective to this book. His contributions helped ensure that the recipes in this collection not only support better health but are backed by scientific understanding.

Together, their combined expertise guarantees that this book is not just a collection of recipes, but a guide to nutritious, satisfying, and health-focused meals. Thank you both for your invaluable support, dedication, and for sharing your knowledge so generously.

TABLE OF CONTENTS

INTRODUCTION

The Magic of Cottage Cheese

Cottage cheese is a powerhouse ingredient, often overlooked but incredibly versatile and nutritious. Its creamy texture and mild flavor make it the perfect addition to both savory and sweet dishes, transforming everyday meals into something special. Whether you're seeking a high-protein breakfast, a light lunch, or a healthy dessert, cottage cheese can fit into virtually any meal. This introduction will take you through the nutritional benefits, varieties, and essential tips for making the most out of this humble ingredient.

Nutritional Benefits

Cottage cheese is a nutrient-dense food that offers several key health benefits, making it a favorite among athletes, dieters, and health-conscious individuals alike. Here's what makes cottage cheese a nutritional superstar:

High in Protein: Cottage cheese is an excellent source of protein, particularly casein, which is a slow-digesting protein that helps keep you full and aids in muscle repair.

Rich in Calcium: Essential for bone health, calcium is abundant in cottage cheese, supporting strong bones and teeth.

Low in Calories: With its high protein content and relatively low calorie count, cottage cheese can be a great choice for those looking to lose weight or maintain a healthy lifestyle.

Good Source of B Vitamins: Cottage cheese contains riboflavin, B12, and other B vitamins that support energy production, brain function, and metabolism.

Gut-Friendly Probiotics: Some varieties of cottage cheese, especially those labeled as "live cultures," can provide probiotics, which support healthy digestion and gut flora.

History and Varieties

Cottage cheese has a long history, dating back to ancient times when milk was naturally fermented and curdled. Over the centuries, it evolved into the creamy, fresh cheese we know today.

It was once considered a "farmhouse cheese," where the curds were made in small batches on farms, and eventually became popular across Europe and North America.

Varieties of Cottage Cheese:

Small Curd vs. Large Curd: These two varieties differ in texture based on the size of the curds. Small-curd cottage cheese tends to be creamier, while large-curd varieties have more noticeable chunks.

Low-Fat vs. Full-Fat: Cottage cheese can range from full-fat (4%) to reduced-fat (2%) to fat-free, offering options for those with different dietary preferences.

Flavored Varieties: Some cottage cheeses come pre-flavored with fruit or herbs, though plain varieties allow for the most versatility in cooking.

How to Choose and Store Cottage Cheese

Choosing the right cottage cheese can make a difference in your recipes. Here are some tips:

Look for Freshness: Check the expiration date and look for cottage cheese with minimal additives or preservatives. The fresher, the better for flavor and texture.

Consider the Fat Content: Full-fat cottage cheese is richer and creamier, perfect for desserts and more indulgent dishes. Low-fat versions work well in smoothies and savory dishes where you don't want the added richness.

Texture Preference: Choose between small curd (creamy, less chunky) and large curd (firmer, more texture) based on the dish you're preparing.

Storage: Always store cottage cheese in the refrigerator. Once opened, keep it tightly sealed and use it within 5 to 7 days for optimal freshness. Stir it before use, as some separation may occur.

Tips for Cooking with Cottage Cheese

Cottage cheese is an incredibly adaptable ingredient, but there are a few tricks to getting the best results when cooking with it:

Drain Excess Liquid: If your recipe calls for a firmer consistency (like in lasagna or stuffed peppers), you may want to drain excess liquid from the cottage cheese by placing it in a strainer or cheesecloth for some few minutes.

Blending for Smoothness: For a smoother texture in dips, smoothies, or desserts, blend the cottage cheese in a food processor or blender until creamy.

Balancing Flavors: Cottage cheese has a naturally mild, slightly tangy flavor. When using it in savory dishes, add herbs, spices, or stronger cheeses like Parmesan to enhance the flavor. For sweet recipes, honey, fruit, or cinnamon are great pairings.

Baking with Cottage Cheese: Cottage cheese can be used in baking for a light and creamy texture.

Try adding it to pancakes, muffins, or casseroles for added moisture and protein.

Substitution: Cottage cheese can sometimes replace ricotta or cream cheese in recipes for a lighter, healthier alternative.

Essential Kitchen Tools

A well-equipped kitchen makes cooking with cottage cheese easier and more enjoyable. Here are the tools you'll need to create the delicious recipes in this book:

Tools and Utensils

Food Processor or Blender: Ideal for blending cottage cheese into smooth bases for dips, smoothies, and sauces.

Cheesecloth or Strainer: To drain excess liquid from cottage cheese when a firmer texture is needed.

Mixing Bowls: For combining ingredients in salads, casseroles, and baked dishes.

Nonstick Skillet: Essential for making cottage cheese pancakes, fritters, or scrambled eggs.

Baking Dishes: Use glass or ceramic dishes for casseroles, lasagna, and baked desserts that feature cottage cheese.

Measuring Cups and Spoons: Accurate measurement is key to getting the best results, especially when baking or making precise recipes.

Hand Mixer or Whisk: Useful for whipping cottage cheese into a light and airy texture for desserts or savory bakes.

Key Ingredients to Pair with Cottage Cheese

Cottage cheese is versatile and pairs beautifully with a wide range of ingredients. Here are some essentials to keep in your kitchen:

Fruits: Berries, peaches, pineapple, and bananas are excellent complements in both fresh and blended forms.

Vegetables: Spinach, tomatoes, cucumbers, and bell peppers bring balance and freshness to savory cottage cheese dishes.

Herbs & Spices: Basil, dill, parsley, and black pepper can enhance the savory flavors, while cinnamon, nutmeg, and vanilla work well in sweet dishes.

Grains: Use oats, quinoa, and whole grains like brown rice to make hearty, protein-rich meals with cottage cheese.

Nuts & Seeds: Almonds, walnuts, chia seeds, and flax seeds add crunch and nutrition to cottage cheese bowls and salads.

Healthy Fats: Avocado, olive oil, and nut butters can make cottage cheese even more satisfying in both savory and sweet applications.

CHAPTER 1: BREAKFAST BOOSTS

Cottage Cheese Pancakes with Fresh Berries

Servings: 4

Prep Time: 10 minutes

Cook Time: 10 minutes

Ingredients:

1 cup cottage cheese

2 eggs

½ cup whole wheat flour

1 tsp baking powder

1 tsp vanilla extract

1 tbsp honey (optional)

Fresh berries (blueberries, strawberries, etc.)

Maple syrup, for serving

Instructions:

1. In a large bowl, combine the cottage cheese, eggs, vanilla extract, and honey.

2. In another basin, add the flour and baking powder. Gently combine the dry ingredients with the wet mixture.

3. Heat a nonstick pan over medium heat and lightly coat with butter or oil.

4. Scoop ¼ cup batter into the pan and cook until bubbles form, approximately 2 minutes per side.

5. Serve warm, with fresh berries and a drizzle of maple syrup.

Nutritional Values (per serving):

Calories: ~200, Protein: 10g, Carbohydrates: 25g, Fat: 8g, Fiber: 3g, Sugars: 6g

Protein-Packed Cottage Cheese Scramble

Servings: 2

<u>Prep Time:</u> 5 minutes

<u>Cook Time:</u> 10 minutes

Ingredients:

3 large eggs

¼ cup cottage cheese

1 cup baby spinach (optional)

¼ cup chopped mushrooms (optional)

Salt and pepper, to taste

Fresh herbs for garnish (chives, parsley)

Instructions:

1. In a bowl, whisk together the eggs and season with salt and pepper.

2. Heat a nonstick skillet over medium heat and sauté mushrooms or spinach, if using.

3. Pour the eggs into the skillet and cook until they begin to set.

4. Fold in the cottage cheese and cook until the eggs are thoroughly scrambled, stirring occasionally.

5. Garnish with fresh herbs and serve alongside whole grain bread or avocado slices.

Nutritional Values (per serving):

Calories: ~250, Protein: 20g, Carbohydrates: 10g, Fat: 15g, Fiber: 2g, Sugars: 2g

Cottage Cheese Overnight Oats

Servings: 1

<u>Prep Time:</u> 5 minutes (plus overnight refrigeration)

Ingredients:

½ cup rolled oats

½ cup cottage cheese

½ cup almond milk (or any milk of choice)

1 tbsp chia seeds

1 tbsp honey or maple syrup

½ tsp vanilla extract

Fresh fruit, nuts, and seeds for topping

Instructions:

1. In a jar or bowl, combine the oats, cottage cheese, almond milk, chia seeds, honey, and vanilla extract.
2. Stir thoroughly, cover, and refrigerate overnight.
3. In the morning, stir and add extra milk as needed to achieve the desired consistency.
4. Garnish with fresh fruit, nuts, or seeds and enjoy.

Nutritional Values (per serving):

Calories: ~350

Protein: 15g

Carbohydrates: 45g

Fat: 10g

Fiber: 7g

Sugars: 15g

Cottage Cheese and Avocado Toast

Servings: 1

Prep Time: 5 minutes

Cook Time: None

Ingredients:

1 slice whole grain or sourdough bread, toasted

¼ cup cottage cheese

½ avocado, mashed

1 tbsp pumpkin or sunflower seeds (optional)

¼ tsp red pepper flakes (optional)

Lemon wedge for serving

Instructions:

1. Toast the bread to your taste.

2. Spread a layer of cottage cheese onto the toast.

3. Mash the avocado and spread it on the cottage cheese.

4. Sprinkle with seeds and red pepper flakes, and finish with a squeeze of fresh lemon.

5. Serve immediately for a satisfying and nutrient-packed breakfast.

Nutritional Values (per serving):

Calories: ~300

Protein: 10g

Carbohydrates: 30g

Fat: 15g

Fiber: 8g

Sugars: 2g

Spinach and Cottage Cheese Breakfast Muffins

Servings: 6

Prep Time: 10 minutes

Cook Time: 20 minutes

Ingredients:

1 cup cottage cheese

1 cup fresh spinach, chopped

4 eggs

¼ cup almond flour (or regular flour)

1 tsp baking powder

¼ cup grated Parmesan cheese (optional)

Salt and pepper, to taste

Instructions:

1. Preheat the oven to 350°F (175°C) and grease a muffin tin.
2. In a mixing dish, whisk the eggs, then fold in the cottage cheese, spinach, almond flour, baking powder, and Parmesan cheese, if desired.
3. Season with salt and pepper.
4. Pour the mixture evenly into the muffin tin and bake for 18-20 minutes, or until the tops are golden and firm.
5. Let cool slightly before serving. Store leftovers in the fridge for up to 4 days.

Nutritional Values (per muffin):

Calories: ~150, Protein: 10g, Carbohydrates: 7g, Fat: 9g, Fiber: 1g, Sugars: 2g

CHAPTER 2: SMOOTHIES & SHAKES

Strawberry Banana Cottage Cheese Smoothie

Servings: 2

Prep Time: 5 minutes

Ingredients:

1 cup cottage cheese

1 banana, sliced

1 cup fresh or frozen strawberries

½ cup almond milk (or any milk)

1 tbsp honey or maple syrup (optional)

Ice cubes (optional)

Instructions:

1. In a blender, combine cottage cheese, banana, strawberries, and almond milk.

2. Blend until smooth. For more sweetness, use honey or maple syrup.

3. Add ice cubes and blend again to achieve a colder, thicker texture.

4. Pour it into a glass and drink immediately.

Nutritional Values (per serving):

Calories: ~250

Protein: 15g

Carbohydrates: 30g

Fat: 5g

Fiber: 4g

Sugars: 18g

Mango Cottage Cheese Protein Shake

Servings: 2

<u>Prep Time:</u> 5 minutes

Ingredients:

1 cup cottage cheese

1 cup fresh or frozen mango chunks

½ cup orange juice

1 scoop vanilla protein powder (optional)

½ tsp ground turmeric (optional for extra health benefits)

Ice cubes (optional)

Instructions:

1. Blend cottage cheese, mango, orange juice, and protein powder.
2. Blend until smooth. If used, add turmeric.
3. Add ice cubes to make the shake thicker, then blend again.
4. Serve immediately for a protein-rich drink.

Nutritional Values (per serving):

Calories: ~280

Protein: 20g

Carbohydrates: 35g

Fat: 5g

Fiber: 3g

Sugars: 28g

Green Detox Smoothie with Cottage Cheese

Servings: 2

Prep Time: 5 minutes

Ingredients:

1 cup cottage cheese

1 cup fresh spinach or kale

½ cucumber, peeled and chopped

1 green apple, cored and chopped

½ lemon, juiced

1 cup water or coconut water

Ice cubes (optional)

Instructions:

1. Blend the cottage cheese, spinach, cucumber, apple, lemon juice, and water until smooth.
2. If desired, add ice cubes and re-blend.
3. Pour into a glass and drink immediately.

Nutritional Values (per serving):

Calories: ~230

Protein: 15g

Carbohydrates: 30g

Fat: 5g

Fiber: 5g

Sugars: 20g

Chocolate Cottage Cheese Protein Shake

Servings: 2

<u>Prep Time:</u> 5 minutes

Ingredients:

1 cup cottage cheese

2 tbsp unsweetened cocoa powder

1 cup milk (any kind)

1-2 tbsp honey or maple syrup (to taste)

1 scoop chocolate protein powder (optional)

Ice cubes (optional)

Instructions:

1. Blend together cottage cheese, cocoa powder, milk, and protein powder (if using) until creamy.
2. Add honey or maple syrup to taste.
3. Add ice cubes to make the shake thicker, then blend again.
4. Serve immediately for a delicious, protein-rich chocolate fix.

Nutritional Values (per serving):

Calories: ~300

Protein: 20g

Carbohydrates: 30g

Fat: 10g

Fiber: 3g

Sugars: 20g

Tropical Cottage Cheese Smoothie Bowl

Servings: 2

<u>Prep Time:</u> 10 minutes

Ingredients:

1 cup cottage cheese

1 cup frozen pineapple chunks

1 banana

½ cup coconut milk

1 tbsp honey or agave syrup (optional)

Toppings:

Fresh mango slices

Kiwi slices

Chia seeds

Shredded coconut

Granola

Instructions:

1. In a blender, combine cottage cheese, pineapple, banana, coconut milk, and honey.
2. Blend until smooth and creamy.
3. Pour into a bowl and top with fresh mango, kiwi slices, chia seeds, shredded coconut, and granola.
4. Enjoy immediately with a spoon.

Nutritional Values (per serving):

Calories: ~350

Protein: 15g

Carbohydrates: 50g

Fat: 10g

Fiber: 6g

Sugars: 30g

CHAPTER 3: APPETIZERS & SNACKS

Cottage Cheese Stuffed Mini Bell Peppers

Servings: 6 (2 mini peppers per serving)

Prep Time: 10 minutes

Cook Time: 20 minutes

Ingredients:

12 mini bell peppers, halved and seeds removed

1 cup cottage cheese

1 tbsp fresh parsley, chopped

1 tbsp fresh dill, chopped

1 garlic clove, minced

Salt and pepper, to taste

Olive oil, for drizzling

Instructions:

1. Preheat the oven to 375°F (190°C).

2. In a bowl, combine the cottage cheese, parsley, dill, garlic, salt, and pepper.

3. Fill each small bell pepper half with cottage cheese mixture.

4. Place the filled peppers on a baking sheet, drizzle with olive oil, and cook for 15-20 minutes, or until slightly softened.

5. Serve warm or at room temperature as a healthy appetizer or snack.

Nutritional Values (per serving):

Calories: ~100, Protein: 5g, Carbohydrates: 7g, Fat: 5g, Fiber: 2g, Sugars: 4g

Crispy Cottage Cheese Fritters with Dipping Sauce

Servings: 4 (3-4 fritters per serving)

Prep Time: 10 minutes

Cook Time: 15 minutes

Ingredients:

1 cup cottage cheese

½ cup breadcrumbs (or almond flour for a low-carb option)

2 eggs

2 tbsp fresh parsley, chopped

1 garlic clove, minced

¼ cup grated Parmesan cheese (optional)

Salt and pepper, to taste

Olive oil, for frying

For the Dipping Sauce:

½ cup Greek yogurt

1 tbsp lemon juice

1 tbsp fresh dill, chopped

Salt and pepper, to taste

Instructions:

1. In a mixing bowl, combine cottage cheese, breadcrumbs, eggs, parsley, garlic, Parmesan (if using), salt, and pepper.
2. Form the mixture into tiny patties.
3. In a large pan, heat the olive oil over medium heat. Fry the fritters for 3-4 minutes on each side, until golden and crispy.
4. Combine the dipping sauce ingredients in a small bowl.
5. Serve the fritters hot, with yogurt dipping sauce on the side.

Nutritional Values (per serving):

Calories: ~250, Protein: 15g, Carbohydrates: 20g, Fat: 12g, Fiber: 2g, Sugars: 2g

Herbed Cottage Cheese Dip with Veggies

Servings: 6 (½ cup dip per serving)

Prep Time: 10 minutes

Cook Time: None

Ingredients:

1½ cups cottage cheese

2 tbsp fresh chives, chopped

1 tbsp fresh dill, chopped

1 tbsp fresh parsley, chopped

1 garlic clove, minced

1 tbsp lemon juice

Salt and pepper, to taste

Assorted raw vegetables (carrots, cucumbers, bell peppers, celery)

Instructions:

1. In a food processor, combine cottage cheese, chives, dill, parsley, garlic, and lemon juice until smooth and creamy.
2. Season with salt and pepper to taste.
3. Transfer the dip to a serving bowl and garnish with additional herbs, if desired.
4. Serve with a variety of raw veggies for dipping.

Nutritional Values (per serving):

Calories: ~120

Protein: 10g

Carbohydrates: 6g

Fat: 6g

Fiber: 1g

Sugars: 3g

Cottage Cheese and Pesto Stuffed Mushrooms

Servings: 6 (2 mushrooms per serving)

Prep Time: 10 minutes

Cook Time: 20 minutes

Ingredients:

12 large white mushrooms, stems removed

1 cup cottage cheese

2 tbsp basil pesto

¼ cup grated Parmesan cheese (optional)

Salt and pepper, to taste

Olive oil, for drizzling

Instructions:

1. Preheat the oven to 375°F (190°C).

2. In a bowl, combine the cottage cheese, pesto, Parmesan (if using), salt, and pepper.

3. Spoon the cottage cheese mixture into each mushroom cap.

4. Place the mushrooms on a baking sheet, spray with olive oil, and bake for 20 minutes, until they are soft and the filling is brown.

5. Serve warm for a flavorful appetizer or snack.

Nutritional Values (per serving):

Calories: ~110, Protein: 8g, Carbohydrates: 5g, Fat: 6g, Fiber: 1g, Sugars: 2g

Cottage Cheese and Olive Tapenade Crostini

Servings: 8 (3 crostini per serving)

Prep Time: 10 minutes

Cook Time: 7 minutes

Ingredients:

1 baguette, sliced into thin rounds

1 cup cottage cheese

½ cup olive tapenade (store-bought or homemade)

Olive oil, for brushing

Fresh basil leaves, for garnish

Instructions:

1. Preheat the oven to 400 °F (200 °C).

2. Brush the baguette slices with olive oil and place them on a baking pan. Bake for 5–7 minutes, or until golden and crispy.

3. Spread a layer of cottage cheese onto each crostini.

4. Finish with a spoonful of olive tapenade and fresh basil leaves.

5. Serve immediately as an appetizer or snack.

Nutritional Values (per serving):

Calories: ~180, Protein: 6g, Carbohydrates: 22g, Fat: 8g, Fiber: 2g, Sugars: 1g

CHAPTER 4: SAVORY MAINS

Cottage Cheese and Spinach Stuffed Chicken Breasts

Servings: 4

Prep Time: 15 minutes

Cook Time: 25-30 minutes

Ingredients:

4 boneless, skinless chicken breasts

1 cup cottage cheese

1 cup fresh spinach, chopped

1 garlic clove, minced

2 tbsp fresh parsley, chopped

½ cup grated mozzarella cheese (optional)

Salt and pepper, to taste

2 tbsp olive oil

Instructions:

1. Preheat the oven to 375°F (190°C).
2. In a bowl, combine the cottage cheese, spinach, garlic, parsley, and mozzarella (if using). Season with salt and pepper.
3. Cut a pocket into each chicken breast by slicing it horizontally, taking care not to cut through.
4. Fill each pocket with cottage cheese mixture and seal with toothpicks.
5. In a large oven-proof skillet, heat the olive oil over medium heat. Sear the chicken breasts for 3-4 minutes per side, until browned.
6. Bake the skillet for 20-25 minutes, or until the chicken is thoroughly done.
7. Serve hot alongside roasted veggies or a fresh salad.

Nutritional Values (per serving):

Calories: ~350, Protein: 42g, Carbohydrates: 4g, Fat: 18g, Fiber: 1g, Sugars: 1g

Vegetable Lasagna with Cottage Cheese

Servings: 6

Prep Time: 20 minutes

Cook Time: 45-50 minutes

Ingredients:

9 lasagna noodles

1½ cups cottage cheese

2 cups marinara sauce

1 zucchini, thinly sliced

1 yellow squash, thinly sliced

1 cup mushrooms, sliced

1½ cups mozzarella cheese, shredded

1 tsp dried oregano

1 tsp dried basil

Salt and pepper, to taste

Olive oil, for roasting

Instructions:

1. Preheat the oven to 375°F (190°C).
2. Mix the zucchini, squash, and mushrooms with olive oil, salt, and pepper. Roast for 15-20 minutes, until tender.
3. Cook your lasagna noodles according to the package instructions.
4. In a bowl, combine cottage cheese, oregano, and basil. Season with salt and pepper.
5. Spread a thin layer of marinara sauce at the bottom of a baking dish. Layer with noodles, roasted vegetables, cottage cheese, and marinara sauce. Repeat layering until all ingredients are utilized, then top with marinara sauce and mozzarella cheese.
6. Cover with a foil and bake for about 30 minutes. Remove the foil and bake for another 10-15 minutes, until the cheese is bubbling and brown.
7. Allow the lasagna to rest for ten minutes before slicing and serving.

Nutritional Values (per serving):

Calories: ~300, Protein: 18g, Carbohydrates: 35g, Fat: 12g, Fiber: 4g, Sugars: 7g

Cottage Cheese and Mushroom Quiche

Servings: 6

Prep Time: 15 minutes

Cook Time: 35-40 minutes

Ingredients:

1 pre-made pie crust (or homemade)

1 cup cottage cheese

1 cup mushrooms, sliced

½ cup grated Gruyère or cheddar cheese

4 large eggs

½ cup milk or cream

1 tbsp olive oil

1 tsp fresh thyme leaves

Salt and pepper, to taste

Instructions:

1. Preheat the oven to 375°F (190°C).

2. In a skillet, heat the olive oil over medium heat. Sauté the mushrooms until brown and soft, about 5-7 minutes. Set aside.

3. In a bowl, combine the eggs, milk, cottage cheese, thyme, salt, and pepper.

4. Put the pie crust in a quiche or pie dish. Spread the sautéed mushrooms equally across the crust.

5. Pour the cottage cheese mixture over the mushrooms and top with Gruyere cheese.

6. Bake for 35-40 minutes, or until the quiche has set and turned golden brown on top.

7. Allow it cool a bit before slicing and serving.

Nutritional Values (per serving):

Calories: ~250, Protein: 14g, Carbohydrates: 15g, Fat: 15g, Fiber: 1g, Sugars: 3g

Cottage Cheese-Stuffed Bell Peppers

Servings: 4

Prep Time: 20 minutes

Cook Time: 30-35 minutes

Ingredients:

4 large bell peppers (any color), tops removed and seeds cleaned out

1 cup cottage cheese

1 cup cooked quinoa

1 cup diced tomatoes

½ cup corn kernels (optional)

1 garlic clove, minced

1 tsp cumin

1 tsp smoked paprika

Salt and pepper, to taste

½ cup shredded cheddar cheese (optional)

Instructions:

1. Preheat the oven to 375°F (190°C).
2. In a bowl, add the cottage cheese, cooked quinoa, tomatoes, corn, garlic, cumin, paprika, salt, and pepper.
3. Stuff each bell pepper with the cottage cheese mixture and set it upright in a baking tray.
4. If desired, add shredded cheddar cheese on top.
5. Bake for 30-35 minutes, until the peppers are tender and the filling is heated through.
6. Serve hot, garnished with fresh herbs or a drizzle of hot sauce.

Nutritional Values (per serving):

Calories: ~280, Protein: 16g, Carbohydrates: 30g, Fat: 12g, Fiber: 6g, Sugars: 8g

Sweet Potato and Cottage Cheese Casserole

Servings: 6

Prep Time: 15 minutes

Cook Time: 45-50 minutes

Ingredients:

2 large sweet potatoes, peeled and sliced thinly

1½ cups cottage cheese

½ cup milk

2 tbsp butter, melted

1 tsp cinnamon

1 tsp nutmeg

¼ cup grated Parmesan cheese (optional)

Salt and pepper, to taste

Instructions:

1. Preheat the oven to 375°F (190°C).
2. In a bowl, combine the cottage cheese, milk, melted butter, cinnamon, nutmeg, salt, and pepper.
3. Place half of the sweet potato slices in a greased baking dish. Spread half of the cottage cheese mixture on top.
4. Repeat with the remaining sweet potatoes and cottage cheese mix.
5. Sprinkle with Parmesan cheese, if using.
6. Cover with a foil and bake for about 30 minutes. Remove the cover and bake for another 15-20 minutes, until the top is golden and the sweet potatoes are soft.
7. Allow to cool slightly before serving.

Nutritional Values (per serving):

Calories: ~220, Protein: 8g, Carbohydrates: 30g, Fat: 8g, Fiber: 4g, Sugars: 10g

CHAPTER 5: LIGHT LUNCHES

Cottage Cheese and Cucumber Sandwich

Servings: 2

Prep Time: 10 minutes

Ingredients:

4 slices whole grain bread

1 cup cottage cheese

1 cucumber, thinly sliced

2 tbsp fresh dill, chopped

1 tbsp lemon juice

Salt and pepper, to taste

Butter or cream cheese (optional, for spreading)

Instructions:

1. In a bowl, combine the cottage cheese, dill, lemon juice, salt, and pepper.

2. Spread butter or cream cheese on one side of each slice of bread, if desired.

3. Spread the cottage cheese mixture evenly on two slices of toast.

4. Layer the cucumber slices on top of the cottage cheese.

5. Top with the remaining bread slices and cut the sandwiches in half or quarters.

6. Serve immediately or wrap for a lunch on-the-go.

Nutritional Values (per serving):

Calories: ~240, Protein: 16g, Carbohydrates: 34g, Fat: 6g, Fiber: 4g, Sugars: 4g

Tuna Salad with Cottage Cheese and Dill

Servings: 2

Prep Time: 10 minutes

Ingredients:

1 can tuna, drained

½ cup cottage cheese

2 tbsp fresh dill, chopped

1 celery stalk, finely diced

1 small red onion, finely diced

1 tbsp lemon juice

Salt and pepper, to taste

Mixed greens or whole-grain crackers, for serving

Instructions:

1. In a mixing dish, add tuna, cottage cheese, dill, celery, red onion, and lemon juice.
2. Season with some salt and pepper to taste.
3. Mix well until all ingredients are well combined.
4. Serve over mixed greens or with whole-grain crackers

Nutritional Values (per serving):

Calories: ~180

Protein: 24g

Carbohydrates: 5g

Fat: 7g

Fiber: 1g

Sugars: 2g

Cottage Cheese and Egg Salad Lettuce Wraps

Servings: 2

Prep Time: 10 minutes

Ingredients:

4 large lettuce leaves (such as Butter Lettuce or Romaine)

4 hard-boiled eggs, chopped

½ cup cottage cheese

2 tbsp fresh chives, chopped

1 tbsp Dijon mustard

Salt and pepper, to taste

Paprika or hot sauce (optional, for garnish)

Instructions:

1. In a bowl, add the chopped eggs, cottage cheese, chives, Dijon mustard, salt, and pepper.
2. Mix until thoroughly combined.
3. Spoon the egg salad mixture over each lettuce leaf.
4. Garnish with paprika or a dash of hot sauce if preferred.
5. Serve immediately for a light and refreshing lunch.

Nutritional Values (per serving):

Calories: ~210

Protein: 18g

Carbohydrates: 3g

Fat: 14g

Fiber: 1g

Sugars: 2g

Cottage Cheese and Roasted Veggie Wrap

Servings: 1

Prep Time: 10 minutes (plus roasting time for veggies)

Cook Time: 20 minutes (for roasting vegetables)

Ingredients:

1 large tortilla or wrap

1 cup cottage cheese

1 cup mixed roasted vegetables (such as bell peppers, zucchini, and carrots)

1 tbsp balsamic vinegar

1 tbsp olive oil

1 tsp dried oregano

Salt and pepper, to taste

Instructions:

1. Spread the cottage cheese evenly across the tortilla.

2. In a mixing bowl, combine the roasted veggies with the balsamic vinegar, olive oil, oregano, salt, and pepper.

3. Spread the roasted vegetables over the cottage cheese.

4. Roll the tortilla tightly, cut in half, and serve.

5. Wrap in foil for a portable lunch, or eat immediately.

Nutritional Values (per serving):

Calories: ~320

Protein: 14g

Carbohydrates: 38g

Fat: 14g

Fiber: 6g

Sugars: 6g

Cottage Cheese and Smoked Salmon on Rye

Servings: 1

<u>Prep Time</u>: 5 minutes

Ingredients:

2 slices rye bread

1 cup cottage cheese

4 oz smoked salmon

1 tbsp capers

1 tbsp fresh dill, chopped

1 tbsp lemon juice

Salt and pepper, to taste

Instructions:

1. Spread the cottage cheese evenly on each slice of rye bread.
2. Top with pieces of smoked salmon.
3. Garnish with capers, fresh dill, and a squeeze of lemon.
4. Season with some salt and pepper to taste.
5. Serve immediately or wrap and refrigerate to use later.

Nutritional Values (per serving):

Calories: ~350

Protein: 28g

Carbohydrates: 20g

Fat: 15g

Fiber: 4g

Sugars: 3g

CHAPTER 6: SIDES & ACCOMPANIMENTS

Garlic Mashed Potatoes with Cottage Cheese

Servings: 4

Prep Time: 10 minutes

Cook Time: 25 minutes

Ingredients:

4 large russet potatoes, peeled and cubed

1 cup cottage cheese

4 garlic cloves, minced

½ cup milk or cream

2 tbsp butter

Salt and pepper, to taste

Fresh chives (optional, for garnish)

Instructions:

1. Boil the potatoes in salted water until soft, about 15-20 minutes. Drain well.

2. In a small saucepan warm and melt the butter and sauté the minced garlic until fragrant, about 1-2 minutes.

3. Mash the cooked potatoes with a potato masher or fork, then add the sautéed garlic, milk, and cottage cheese.

4. Season with salt and pepper, adjusting consistency with more milk if needed.

5. Garnish with fresh chives if desired, and serve hot.

Nutritional Values (per serving):

Calories: ~220 kcal, Protein: 9g, Carbohydrates: 35g, Fat: 7g, Fiber: 3g, Sodium: 180mg

Roasted Sweet Potatoes with Cottage Cheese Drizzle

Servings: 4

Prep Time: 10 minutes

Cook Time: 30 minutes

Ingredients:

4 medium sweet potatoes, sliced into wedges

2 tbsp olive oil

1 tsp smoked paprika

1 tsp cumin

Salt and pepper, to taste

¾ cup cottage cheese

2 tbsp lemon juice

2 tbsp fresh parsley, chopped (optional, for garnish)

Instructions:

1. Preheat the oven to 400 °F (200 °C).

2. Toss the sweet potato wedges with olive oil, paprika, cumin, salt, and pepper.

3. Spread in a single layer on a baking sheet, then roast for 25-30 minutes, flipping halfway through, until soft and golden.

4. While the sweet potatoes roast, combine the cottage cheese and lemon juice until smooth.

5. Once the sweet potatoes are done, drizzle with the cottage cheese sauce and garnish with fresh parsley.

6. Serve warm as a side to grilled meats or a light salad.

Nutritional Values (per serving):

Calories: ~180 kcal, Protein: 5g, Carbohydrates: 28g, Fat: 6g, Fiber: 4g, Sodium: 210mg

Cottage Cheese and Chive Potato Salad

Servings: 6

Prep Time: 15 minutes

Cook Time: 15 minutes

Ingredients:

2 lbs small red potatoes, boiled and halved

1 cup cottage cheese

¼ cup sour cream or Greek yogurt

2 tbsp Dijon mustard

2 tbsp apple cider vinegar

¼ cup fresh chives, chopped

Salt and pepper, to taste

1 small red onion, finely chopped (optional)

Instructions:

1. Boil the potatoes in salted water for 15 minutes, or until they are fork-tender. Drain and cool gently.

2. In a bowl, combine the cottage cheese, sour cream, Dijon mustard, apple cider vinegar, salt, and pepper.

3. Toss the warm potatoes with the cottage cheese dressing, carefully tossing to combine.

4. Add chopped chives and red onion (if using), and adjust seasoning with salt and pepper.

5. Serve chilled or at room temperature, perfect for picnics or barbecues.

Nutritional Values (per serving):

Calories: ~150 kcal, Protein: 6g, Carbohydrates: 25g, Fat: 4g, Fiber: 3g, Sodium: 160mg

Cottage Cheese Mashed Cauliflower

Servings: 4

Prep Time: 10 minutes

Cook Time: 15 minutes

Ingredients:

1 large head of cauliflower, cut into florets

1 cup cottage cheese

2 tbsp butter

½ cup milk or cream

2 garlic cloves, minced

Salt and pepper, to taste

Fresh parsley (optional, for garnish)

Instructions:

1. Steam or boil the cauliflower florets for 10 minutes, or until soft. Drain well.

2. In a skillet, melt butter and cook garlic until fragrant.

3. In a blender or food processor, combine cooked cauliflower, cottage cheese, garlic butter, and milk. Blend until smooth and creamy.

4. Season with some salt and pepper, and adjust consistency with more milk if necessary.

5. Garnish with fresh parsley and serve hot as a low-carb side option.

Nutritional Values (per serving):

Calories: ~130 kcal, Protein: 7g, Carbohydrates: 12g, Fat: 8g, Fiber: 4g, Sodium: 160mg

Cottage Cheese and Dill Biscuits

Servings: 8 biscuits

Prep Time: 15 minutes

Cook Time: 15 minutes

Ingredients:

2 cups all-purpose flour

1 tbsp baking powder

½ tsp baking soda

1 tsp salt

½ cup cold butter, cubed

1 cup cottage cheese

2 tbsp fresh dill, chopped

½ cup milk or buttermilk

Instructions:

1. Preheat the oven to 425°F (220°C). Line a baking sheet with parchment paper.
2. In a large bowl, whisk together flour, baking powder, baking soda, and salt.
3. Cut the chilled butter into the flour mixture with a pastry cutter or your hands until it resembles coarse crumbs.
4. Stir in cottage cheese, dill, and milk until just combined. Be careful not to overmix.
5. Drop the dough by spoonfuls onto the prepared baking sheet, leaving space between each biscuit.
6. Bake for 12-15 minutes, until golden brown and well done.
7. Serve warm, with butter or as an accompaniment to a savory dish.

Nutritional Values (per biscuit):

Calories: ~170 kcal, Protein: 6g, Carbohydrates: 22g, Fat: 7g, Fiber: 1g, Sodium: 300mg

CHAPTER 7: SWEET TREATS & DESSERTS

Cottage Cheese Cheesecake

Servings: 8

<u>Prep Time:</u> 20 minutes

<u>Cook Time:</u> 50-60 minutes

Ingredients:

2 cups cottage cheese

1 cup cream cheese, softened

¾ cup sugar

3 large eggs

1 tsp vanilla extract

1 tbsp lemon juice

1 cup graham cracker crumbs

¼ cup butter, melted

Instructions:

1. Preheat the oven to 325°F (160°C). Grease a 9-inch springform pan.

2. In a bowl, combine the graham cracker crumbs and melted butter. Press the mixture into the bottom of the springform pan to make the crust.

3. In a blender or food processor, puree the cottage cheese until smooth.

4. In a large mixing bowl, combine the cream cheese and sugar. Beat until light and fluffy. Combine the cottage cheese, eggs, vanilla essence, and lemon juice; stir until smooth.

5. Pour the batter over the prepared crust and level the surface.

6. Bake for 50-60 minutes, or until the center is just set. Let cool completely before refrigerating for at least 4 hours.

7. Serve chilled with fresh berries or a drizzle of honey.

Nutritional Values (per serving):

Calories: ~320 kcal, Protein: 10g, Carbohydrates: 30g, Fat: 20g, Fiber: 0.5g, Sodium: 300mg

Lemon Cottage Cheese Pancakes

Servings: 4 (12 pancakes)

Prep Time: 10 minutes

Cook Time: 15 minutes

Ingredients:

1 cup cottage cheese

2 large eggs

1 cup all-purpose flour

1 tbsp sugar

1 tsp baking powder

½ tsp baking soda

Zest of 1 lemon

2 tbsp lemon juice

1 tsp vanilla extract

¼ cup milk

Butter, for cooking

Instructions:

1. In a bowl, combine the flour, sugar, baking powder, and baking soda.

2. In another bowl, combine cottage cheese, eggs, lemon zest, lemon juice, vanilla, and milk until blended.

3. Gradually add the dry ingredients to the wet ingredients, stirring just until combined.

4. Heat a griddle or non-stick skillet over medium heat and melt a small amount of butter.

5. Pour ¼ cup of batter for each pancake, cooking for 2-3 minutes per side, until golden brown.

6. Serve with powdered sugar, maple syrup, or fresh berries for a sweet, citrusy treat.

Nutritional Values (per serving):

Calories: ~250 kcal, Protein: 12g, Carbohydrates: 30g, Fat: 9g

Fiber: 1g, Sodium: 350mg

Baked Cottage Cheese Pudding

Servings: 6

Prep Time: 10 minutes

Cook Time: 30-35 minutes

Ingredients:

1 ½ cups cottage cheese

½ cup sugar

3 large eggs

1 tsp vanilla extract

½ cup milk

¼ cup raisins (optional)

1 tsp cinnamon (optional)

1 tbsp butter, for greasing

Instructions:

1. Preheat the oven to 350°F (175°C).

2. Grease a baking dish with butter.

3. In a blender or food processor, puree the cottage cheese until smooth.

4. In a bowl, combine the eggs, sugar, vanilla extract, and milk. Stir in the blended cottage cheese.

5. Add raisins and cinnamon if desired, and mix until well combined.

6. Pour the mixture into the prepared baking dish and smooth the top.

7. Bake for 30-35 minutes, or until the pudding is set and lightly golden on top.

8. Allow to cool slightly before serving. Enjoy warm or chilled.

Nutritional Values (per serving):

Calories: ~160 kcal, Protein: 10g, Carbohydrates: 18g, Fat: 6g, Fiber: 0.5g, Sodium: 120mg

Chocolate Cottage Cheese Mousse

Servings: 4

Prep Time: 10 minutes

Chill Time: 30 minutes

Ingredients:

1 cup cottage cheese

½ cup dark chocolate, melted

2 tbsp cocoa powder

2 tbsp honey or maple syrup

1 tsp vanilla extract

½ cup whipped cream or coconut cream (optional, for topping)

Instructions:

1. Blend together cottage cheese, melted dark chocolate, cocoa powder, honey, and vanilla extract. Blend until smooth and creamy.

2. Taste and adjust the sweetness as needed by adding more honey or syrup.

3. Transfer the mousse to serving dishes and chill for at least 30 minutes until set.

4. Top with whipped cream or coconut cream for extra indulgence, and garnish with shaved chocolate or fresh berries if desired.

Nutritional Values (per serving):

Calories: ~210 kcal, Protein: 10g, Carbohydrates: 16g, Fat: 12g, Fiber: 2g, Sodium: 150mg

Cottage Cheese and Berry Parfait

Servings: 4

Prep Time: 10 minutes

Total Time: 10 minutes

Ingredients:

1 ½ cups cottage cheese

2 cups mixed fresh berries (such as strawberries, blueberries, and raspberries)

1 cup granola

2 tbsp honey or maple syrup

Fresh mint leaves (optional, for garnish)

Instructions:

1. Place ¼ cup of cottage cheese at the bottom of each serving glass or bowl.
2. Add a layer of fresh berries, then granola.
3. Drizzle some honey or maple syrup over the fruit.
4. Repeat the layers, topping with berries and a drizzle of honey.
5. Garnish with fresh mint leaves if preferred and serve immediately.

Nutritional Values (per serving):

Calories: ~180 kcal

Protein: 10g

Carbohydrates: 28g

Fat: 5g

Fiber: 4g

Sodium: 160mg

CHAPTER 8: LOW-CARB & KETO-FRIENDLY

Keto Cottage Cheese Pancakes

Servings: 4 (makes about 8 pancakes)

Prep Time: 10 minutes

Cook Time: 10-15 minutes

Ingredients:

1 cup cottage cheese

3 large eggs

1 cup almond flour

1 tsp baking powder

½ tsp vanilla extract

Pinch of salt

Butter or coconut oil, for cooking

Instructions:

1. Whisk together the cottage cheese, eggs, and vanilla extract until smooth.
2. In another bowl, combine the almond flour, baking powder, and salt.
3. Mix together the wet and dry ingredients and stir.
4. Heat a nonstick skillet over medium heat, then add a tiny amount of butter or coconut oil.
5. Pour ¼ cup batter for each pancake and heat for 2-3 minutes per side until golden brown.
6. Serve warm, with sugar-free syrup or fresh berries.

Nutritional Values (per serving):

Calories: ~250 kcal

Protein: 10g

Carbohydrates: 8g

Fat: 20g

Fiber: 3g

Sodium: 300mg

Cottage Cheese Egg Bites

Servings: 12 (mini muffins)

Prep Time: 10 minutes

Cook Time: 20-25 minutes

Ingredients:

1 cup cottage cheese

6 large eggs

½ cup shredded cheddar cheese

1 cup cooked spinach, that has been squeezed dry and chopped

½ cup diced bell peppers

1 tsp dried oregano

Salt and pepper, to taste

Instructions:

1. Preheat the oven to 350°F (175°C). Grease a muffin tin or line with paper liners.

2. In a bowl, whisk together the eggs and cottage cheese until well combined.

3. Mix in the shredded cheddar cheese, chopped spinach, diced bell peppers, oregano, salt, and pepper.

4. Divide the mixture equally among the muffin tin cups.

5. Bake for 20-25 minutes, or until the egg bites are set and lightly golden.

6. Let cool slightly before removing from the tin. Enjoy warm or cold.

Nutritional Values (per bite):

Calories: ~80 kcal, Protein: 6g, Carbohydrates: 2g, Fat: 5g

Fiber: 0.5g, Sodium: 180mg

Cottage Cheese and Bacon Casserole

Servings: 6

Prep Time: 10 minutes

Cook Time: 30-35 minutes

Ingredients:

8 oz bacon, cooked and crumbled

1 cup cottage cheese

1 cup shredded mozzarella cheese

4 large eggs

1 cup cooked broccoli florets

1 tsp dried thyme

Salt and pepper, to taste

Instructions:

1. Preheat the oven to 375°F (190°C). Grease a baking dish.
2. In a bowl, combine the cottage cheese, mozzarella cheese, eggs, cooked broccoli, thyme, salt, and pepper.
3. Fold in the crumbled bacon.
4. Pour the mixture into the prepared baking dish and smooth the top.
5. Bake for about 30–35 minutes, or until the casserole is firm and brown.
6. Allow to cool slightly before serving.

Nutritional Values (per serving):

Calories: ~300 kcal

Protein: 20g

Carbohydrates: 6g

Fat: 22g

Fiber: 2g

Sodium: 500mg

Cottage Cheese Cloud Bread

Servings: 6 (mounds)

<u>Prep Time:</u> 10 minutes

<u>Cook Time:</u> 25-30 minutes

Ingredients:

3 large eggs, separated

1 cup cottage cheese

¼ tsp cream of tartar

1 tbsp almond flour

1 tbsp olive oil

1 tbsp fresh chives or parsley (optional, for flavor)

Salt and pepper, to taste

Instructions:

1. Preheat the oven to 300°F/150°C. Line a baking sheet with some parchment paper.

2. In a large mixing bowl, combine the egg whites and cream of tartar. Beat until stiff peaks form.

3. In another bowl, combine the egg yolks, cottage cheese, almond flour, olive oil, salt, and pepper.

4. Gently fold the egg whites into the egg yolk until they are just combined.

5. Drop spoonfuls of the mixture onto the prepared baking sheet, forming 6-8 mounds.

6. Bake for 25-30 minutes, or until the cloud bread is golden brown and firm to the touch.

7. Let cool before using as bread or serving with your meal.

Nutritional Values (per piece):

Calories: ~70 kcal, Protein: 5g, Carbohydrates: 2g, Fat: 5g, Fiber: 0g, Sodium: 120mg

Zucchini Cottage Cheese Fritters

Servings: 4 (makes about 8 fritters)

Prep Time: 15 minutes

Cook Time: 15-20 minutes

Ingredients:

2 medium zucchinis, grated with the excess moisture squeezed out

1 cup cottage cheese

2 large eggs

½ cup almond flour

¼ cup grated Parmesan cheese

2 tbsp fresh parsley, chopped

1 clove garlic, minced

Salt and pepper, to taste

Olive oil or coconut oil, for frying

Instructions:

1. In a bowl, combine grated zucchini, cottage cheese, eggs, almond flour, Parmesan cheese, parsley, garlic, salt, and pepper.
2. Heat a skillet over medium heat and add a small amount of olive oil or coconut oil.
3. Drop spoonfuls of the mixture into the skillet, flattening slightly with the back of the spoon.
4. Cook for 3-4 minutes on each side, or until golden brown and heated through.
5. Drain on paper towels, then serve warm.

Nutritional Values (per fritter):

Calories: ~90 kcal, Protein: 6g, Carbohydrates: 4g, Fat: 6g, Fiber: 1g, Sodium: 150mg

CHAPTER 9: VEGETARIAN & VEGAN OPTIONS

Vegan Cottage Cheese Substitute Recipe

Servings: 4 (about 1 ½ cups)

Prep Time: 10 minutes (plus 4 hours soaking time for cashews)

Ingredients:

1 cup raw cashews, soaked for about 4 hours

½ block firm tofu, crumbled

2 tbsp lemon juice

1 tbsp apple cider vinegar

1 tbsp nutritional yeast

½ tsp garlic powder

½ tsp onion powder

Salt and pepper, to taste

¼ cup unsweetened almond milk (or any other plant-based milk)

Instructions:

1. Drain the soaked cashews and transfer them to a blender or food processor.
2. Combine the lemon juice, apple cider vinegar, nutritional yeast, garlic and onion powders, salt, pepper, and almond milk.
3. Blend until smooth and creamy, scraping down the sides as necessary.
4. Transfer to a bowl and fold in the crumbled tofu to create the texture of cottage cheese.
5. Season to taste. Refrigerate for at least 30 minutes. This is to allow the flavors to combine.
6. Use this vegan cottage cheese substitute in any recipe calling for cottage cheese, or enjoy it as a dip or spread.

Nutritional Values (per serving):

Calories: ~150 kcal, Protein: 6g, Carbohydrates: 8g, Fat: 12g

Fiber: 2g, Sodium: 150mg

Vegetarian Lasagna with Cottage Cheese

Servings: 6

Prep Time: 25 minutes

Cook Time: 35 minutes

Ingredients:

9 lasagna noodles (gluten-free or whole wheat if preferred)

2 cups cottage cheese

1 ½ cups shredded mozzarella cheese

1 jar marinara sauce (about 24 oz)

1 large zucchini, thinly sliced

1 large eggplant, thinly sliced

1 cup fresh spinach

2 cloves garlic, minced

1 tbsp olive oil

Salt and pepper, to taste

Fresh basil, for garnish

Instructions:

1. Preheat the oven to 375°F (190°C).
2. Cook the lasagna noodles according to package instructions, drain, and put aside.
3. Heat the olive oil in a skillet, over medium heat. Add the minced garlic, zucchini, and eggplant slices. Sauté for 5–7 minutes, or until softened. Season with salt and pepper.
4. Spread a thin layer of marinara sauce across the bottom of a 9x13-inch baking dish.
5. Layer 3 lasagna noodles, half of the cottage cheese, half of the sautéed veggies, and a handful of spinach. Top with marinara sauce and a sprinkle of mozzarella cheese.
6. Repeat the layers once more, ending with a layer of noodles, marinara sauce, and remaining mozzarella cheese.
7. Cover the dish with foil and bake for 25 min. Remove the foil and bake for another 10 minutes, or until the cheese is bubbling and brown.
8. Rest for 10 minutes before slicing. Garnish with fresh basil and serve.

Nutritional Values (per serving):

Calories: ~400 kcal, Protein: 22g, Carbohydrates: 45g, Fat: 18g, Fiber: 7g, Sodium: 500mg

Cottage Cheese and Lentil Meatballs

Servings: 4 (makes about 12 meatballs)

Prep Time: 15 minutes

Cook Time: 10 minutes

Ingredients:

1 cup cooked lentils

½ cup cottage cheese

½ cup breadcrumbs (use gluten-free if needed)

1 large egg

1 tsp dried oregano

1 tsp smoked paprika

2 cloves garlic, minced

2 tbsp fresh parsley, chopped

Salt and pepper, to taste

Olive oil, for frying

Instructions:

1. In a mixing bowl, add cooked lentils, cottage cheese, breadcrumbs, egg, oregano, smoked paprika, garlic, parsley, salt, and pepper.
2. Mash the mixture until it holds together while retaining some lentil texture.
3. Roll the mixture into 1-1 ½ inch diameter balls.
4. Heat a skillet over medium heat and add the olive oil. Fry the meatballs for 4-5 minutes per side, until golden brown and crispy.
5. Drain on paper towels before serving with marinara sauce or on a sandwich.

Nutritional Values (per serving):

Calories: ~220 kcal

Protein: 15g

Carbohydrates: 25g

Fat: 7g

Fiber: 7g

Sodium: 300mg

Cottage Cheese Veggie Stuffed Peppers

Servings: 4 (one pepper per person)

Prep Time: 20 minutes

Cook Time: 40 minutes

Ingredients:

4 large bell peppers, tops cut off and seeds removed

1 cup cottage cheese

1 cup cooked quinoa

1 small zucchini, diced

1 small onion, diced

1 cup diced tomatoes

1 tsp cumin

1 tsp paprika

1 tbsp olive oil

Salt and pepper, to taste

Fresh cilantro or parsley, for garnish

Instructions:

1. Preheat the oven to 375°F (190°C). Grease a baking dish.
2. In a skillet, heat the olive oil over medium heat. Sauté the diced onion and zucchini until softened, about 5 minutes.
3. In a bowl, combine the cottage cheese, cooked quinoa, sautéed vegetables, diced tomatoes, cumin, paprika, salt, and pepper.
4. Stuff each bell pepper with the cottage cheese mixture and place in a baking dish.
5. Cover with foil and bake for about 30 minutes. Remove the foil and bake for another 10 minutes, or until the peppers are cooked.
6. Garnish with fresh cilantro or parsley before serving.

Nutritional Values (per serving):

Calories: ~250 kcal

Protein: 15g

Carbohydrates: 30g

Fat: 8g

Fiber: 8g

Sodium: 400mg

Cottage Cheese and Spinach Stuffed Zucchini

Servings: 4 (one zucchini half per person)

Prep Time: 15 minutes

Cook Time: 25-30 minutes

Ingredients:

4 medium zucchinis, that is halved lengthwise and seeds scooped out

1 cup cottage cheese

1 cup fresh spinach, chopped

¼ cup grated Parmesan cheese

1 clove garlic, minced

1 tbsp olive oil

Salt and pepper, to taste

Red pepper flakes (optional)

Instructions:

1. Preheat the oven to 375°F (190°C).
2. Heat olive oil in a skillet over medium heat, then sauté garlic for 1-2 minutes. Add the spinach and then cook for about 3 minutes, or until wilted. Season with salt and pepper.
3. In a bowl, combine the cottage cheese, sautéed spinach, and Parmesan cheese.
4. Spoon the cottage cheese mixture into the hollowed out zucchini halves and place on a baking sheet.
5. Bake for 25–30 minutes, or until the zucchinis are soft and the tops are gently brown.
6. Sprinkle with red pepper flakes for a bit of heat, and serve warm.

Nutritional Values (per serving):

Calories: ~180 kcal

Protein: 10g

Carbohydrates: 8g

Fat: 12g

Fiber: 3g

Sodium: 250mg

BONUS CHAPTER: GLOBAL FLAVORS

Italian-Style Cottage Cheese Lasagna

Servings: 6

Prep Time: 25 minutes

Cook Time: 35 minutes

Ingredients:

9 lasagna noodles (whole wheat or gluten-free)

2 cups cottage cheese

1 ½ cups shredded mozzarella cheese

1 cup grated Parmesan cheese

1 jar marinara sauce (about 24 oz)

1 tbsp olive oil

1 medium onion, diced

3 cloves garlic, minced

1 cup mushrooms, sliced

2 cups fresh spinach

Salt and pepper, to taste

Fresh basil, for garnish

1. Preheat the oven to 375°F (190°C).

2. Cook the lasagna noodles according to package instructions, then drain and put aside.

3. Heat the olive oil in a skillet over medium heat. Sauté the onion, garlic, and mushrooms for 5-7 minutes, until softened. Add the spinach and cook until wilted. Season with salt and pepper.

4. Spread a thin layer of marinara sauce at the bottom of a 9x13-inch baking dish.

5. Layer 3 lasagna noodles, ⅓ of the sautéed veggies, ⅓ of the cottage cheese, marinara sauce, and sprinkle with mozzarella and Parmesan cheese.

6. Repeat the layers twice more, ending with a top layer of noodles, sauce, and cheese.

7. Cover with foil and bake for about 25 minutes.

8. Cover with foil and bake for 25 minutes. Remove the foil and then bake for an extra 10 minutes, until the cheese is bubbly and golden.

9. Let rest for 10 minutes before serving. Garnish with fresh basil.

Nutritional Values (per serving):

Calories: ~450 kcal, Protein: 27g, Carbohydrates: 45g, Fat: 22g, Fiber: 6g, Sodium: 650mg

Mexican-Style Cottage Cheese Stuffed Peppers

Servings: 4 (one pepper per person)

Prep Time: 20 minutes

Cook Time: 40 minutes

Ingredients:

4 large bell peppers, tops cut off and seeds removed

1 cup cottage cheese

1 cup black beans, drained and rinsed

1 cup cooked quinoa or rice

1 tsp cumin

1 tsp smoked paprika

1 tsp chili powder

1 cup corn kernels (fresh or frozen)

½ cup salsa

½ cup shredded cheddar cheese

Fresh cilantro, for garnish

Instructions:

1. Preheat the oven to 375°F (190°C). Grease a baking dish.

2. In a bowl, combine the cottage cheese, black beans, cooked quinoa or rice, cumin, smoked paprika, chili powder, corn, and salsa. Season with salt and pepper.

3. Fill each bell pepper with the mixture and place in the prepared baking dish.

4. Cover with foil and bake for about 30 minutes. Remove the foil, sprinkle the tops with cheddar cheese, and bake for another 10 minutes, or until melted and bubbling.

5. Garnish with fresh cilantro and serve with extra salsa or guacamole.

Nutritional Values (per serving):

Calories: ~320 kcal, Protein: 20g, Carbohydrates: 35g, Fat: 12g, Fiber: 8g, Sodium: 500mg

Indian Paneer Substitute: Cottage Cheese Masala

Servings: 4

Prep Time: 15 minutes

Cook Time: 30 minutes

Ingredients:

2 cups cottage cheese, drained well

1 tbsp ghee or vegetable oil

1 medium onion, finely chopped

2 cloves garlic, minced

1-inch piece ginger, grated

1 can (14 oz) crushed tomatoes

1 tsp cumin seeds

1 tsp ground turmeric

1 tsp garam masala

1 tsp ground coriander

1 tsp chili powder (adjust to taste)

½ cup coconut milk or heavy cream

Fresh cilantro, for garnish

Instructions:

1. In a large skillet, melt ghee or vegetable oil over medium heat. Add the cumin seeds and allow them to sizzle for a few seconds.
2. Sauté chopped onions till golden brown, about 5-7 minutes.
3. Add the garlic and ginger and cook for another 1-2 minutes, or until fragrant.
4. Add crushed tomatoes, turmeric, garam masala, coriander, and chili powder. Simmer the sauce for 10-12 minutes until it thickens and the oil starts to separate.
5. Stir in the cottage cheese, making sure to coat it well with the sauce. Reduce heat and let it simmer for about 5-7 minutes, allowing the flavors to meld.
6. Add coconut milk or cream, and simmer for another 3-5 minutes until the sauce is creamy.
7. Garnish with fresh cilantro and serve hot with basmati rice or naan bread.

Nutritional Values (per serving):

Calories: ~350 kcal, Protein: 20g, Carbohydrates: 15g, Fat: 22g, Fiber: 4g, Sodium: 450mg

Greek Cottage Cheese Spanakopita

Servings: 6

Prep Time: 20 minutes

Cook Time: 50 minutes

Ingredients:

1 pack phyllo dough (thawed)

2 cups cottage cheese

1 lb fresh spinach, chopped

1 small onion, finely diced

2 cloves garlic, minced

2 eggs, beaten

1 tbsp olive oil

Salt and pepper, to taste

½ cup melted butter or olive oil, for brushing phyllo

Instructions:

1. Preheat the oven to 350°F (175°C).
2. Heat olive oil in a skillet over medium heat. Add the diced onion and garlic and then sauté until soft and fragrant. Add chopped spinach and cook until wilted. Remove from heat and let cool.
3. In a bowl, mix cottage cheese, cooked spinach mixture, and beaten eggs. Season with salt and pepper.
4. In a bowl, combine the cottage cheese, cooked spinach combination, and beaten eggs. Season with salt and pepper.
5. Brush a baking dish with melted butter or olive oil. Layer 2 sheets of phyllo dough, brushing each with butter/oil. Repeat this same process until you have 6-8 layers.
6. Spread the spinach and cottage cheese mixture evenly over the phyllo layers. Top with more phyllo, again brushing each layer with butter/oil, until you have 6-8 layers on top.
7. Score the top layers into squares or diamonds using a sharp knife.
8. Bake for 45-50 minutes until the top is golden and crisp. Allow it to cool slightly before cutting and serving.

Nutritional Values (per serving):

Calories: ~300 kcal, Protein: 14g, Carbohydrates: 25g, Fat: 18g, Fiber: 3g, Sodium: 400mg

Japanese Cottage Cheese and Avocado Sushi Rolls

Servings: 4 (makes 4 rolls, about 8 pieces per roll)

Prep Time: 20 minutes

Total Time: 20 minutes

Ingredients:

1 cup sushi rice, cooked and seasoned

4 sheets nori (seaweed)

1 cup cottage cheese

1 ripe avocado, sliced

1 cucumber, julienned

1 tbsp rice vinegar

Soy sauce, for serving

Pickled ginger and wasabi (optional)

Instructions:

1. Prepare the sushi rice by cooking it according to package directions. Season with rice vinegar and cool to room temperature.
2. Place a sheet of nori, shiny side down, on a bamboo sushi mat.
3. Spread a thin, even layer of sushi rice over the nori, leaving a 1-inch strip on top.
4. Place a line of cottage cheese, avocado slices, and cucumber in the center of the rice.
5. Roll the sushi tightly using the bamboo mat, pressing gently to form a firm roll. Seal the edge with a little water on the strip of nori.
6. Slice the roll into bite-sized pieces using a sharp knife.
7. Serve with soy sauce, pickled ginger, and wasabi if desired.

Nutritional Values (per serving):

Calories: ~220 kcal, Protein: 12g, Carbohydrates: 30g, Fat: 8g

Fiber: 5g, Sodium: 300mg

Shopping List Essentials

Dairy & Dairy Alternatives:

Cottage cheese (regular, low-fat, and fat-free)

Mozzarella cheese (shredded)

Parmesan cheese (grated)

Cheddar cheese (shredded)

Cream cheese (for desserts)

Butter (or dairy-free alternatives like coconut oil)

Eggs (or egg substitutes)

Almond milk (for dairy-free options)

Coconut milk or cream

Non-dairy cheese alternatives (for vegan recipes)

Fresh Produce:

Avocados

Bell peppers (red, yellow, and green)

Spinach (fresh)

Cucumbers

Tomatoes

Zucchini

Mushrooms (button or cremini)

Sweet potatoes

Onions (yellow, red, and green)

Garlic

Fresh herbs (basil, parsley, cilantro, dill)

Lemons and limes

Strawberries

Blueberries

Bananas

Mangoes

Apples

Baby carrots

Celery

Mixed greens (arugula, lettuce, etc.)

Cabbage (for slaws or wraps)

Grains & Baking Staples:

Whole wheat or gluten-free flour

Almond flour (for keto and low-carb recipes)

Baking powder

Baking soda

Quinoa

Rolled oats (regular or gluten-free)

Phyllo dough (for spanakopita)

Whole wheat or gluten-free pasta (for lasagna)

Rye bread or whole wheat bread

Tortillas (whole wheat or gluten-free)

Nori sheets (for sushi rolls)

Meat & Seafood:

Chicken breasts

Ground turkey or beef

Bacon (or turkey bacon for leaner options)

Smoked salmon

Tuna (canned or fresh)

Canned & Packaged Goods:

Black beans (canned)

Chickpeas (canned)

Diced tomatoes (canned)

Crushed tomatoes (canned)

Salsa

Vegetable broth

Tomato paste

Pesto sauce

Olives (green and Kalamata)

Olive tapenade

Pickled ginger (for sushi)

Soy sauce (or tamari for gluten-free)

Nuts, Seeds & Sweeteners:

Almonds

Cashews (for dairy-free cheese alternatives)

Chia seeds

Flaxseeds

Pumpkin seeds

Sunflower seeds

Sesame seeds

Honey

Maple syrup

Coconut sugar

Agave syrup (for vegan-friendly sweetener)

Spices & Seasonings:

Salt and pepper

Cumin

Smoked paprika

Chili powder

Turmeric

Garam masala (for Indian-inspired dishes)

Ground coriander

Ground cinnamon

Ground nutmeg

Garlic powder

Onion powder

Italian seasoning

Fresh dill or dried dill

Crushed red pepper flakes

Oils & Fats:

Olive oil

Coconut oil

Ghee (for Indian dishes)

Vegetable oil

Avocado oil

Cooking spray (for baking)

Baking & Dessert Ingredients:

Cocoa powder (unsweetened)

Dark chocolate (for mousse)

Vanilla extract

Gelatin (for puddings and cheesecakes)

Lemon juice and zest

Graham crackers (for cheesecake crusts or gluten-free versions)

Almond butter (or other nut butters for snacks and desserts)

CONCLUSION:

Cottage Cheese in Everyday Cooking

Cottage cheese, once considered a simple diet food, has proven itself to be an incredibly versatile and nutrient-dense ingredient that can be incorporated into all types of dishes, from breakfast boosts and sweet treats to savory mains and global flavors. Whether you're looking to add protein to a meal, create creamy textures without added fat, or simply enjoy a new way to elevate your favorite recipes, cottage cheese offers endless possibilities.

In this book, we've explored the magic of cottage cheese across various cuisines and culinary styles. From its creamy addition to pancakes and smoothies to its starring role in lasagna and casseroles, cottage cheese has proven to be a staple ingredient that enhances both flavor and nutrition. Its mild taste makes it the perfect blank canvas for both sweet and savory applications, while its rich texture adds substance to a variety of meals.

Final Thoughts

As you bring cottage cheese into your daily cooking, remember that it's an ingredient that shines both on its own and as part of larger dishes. Whether you're meal-prepping for the week, making a hearty breakfast, or crafting an elegant dinner for guests, cottage cheese offers a nutritious and delicious option for every meal. Continue experimenting with substitutions, pairing it with your favorite ingredients, and exploring global flavors to make cottage cheese a versatile staple in your kitchen.

Happy Cooking!

Made in the USA
Monee, IL
02 January 2025

75827674R00075